A Day at the Beach

Pete, Jem and Belle are enjoying a day at the beach until the weather turns stormy.

Targeting Subject-Verb-Object sentences and early adjectives, this book provides repea[...]
ing syntax and morphology which will engage and excite the reader while building pre-l[...] ...iaking learn-
ing fun. It also exposes the reader to multiple models of the target grammar form.

Perfect for a speech and language therapy session, this book is an ideal starting point for targeting client goals and can also be enjoyed at school or at home to reinforce what has been taught in the therapy session.

Jessica Habib studied speech pathology at the University of Sydney, graduating in 2012. She has since worked with children in indigenous health, community, private, not-for-profit and education settings in both Australia and the UK. Jessica loves the privilege she has of seeing children thrive as they are guided to build and strengthen their communication skills.

Carina Ward is an illustrator based in the Blue Mountains, Australia. She works with watercolour and ink to create beautiful, bright images and likes to add a touch of humour to her work. Carina loves the way pictures tell stories and open up imaginary worlds.

What's in the pack?

A Day at the Beach

A *Grammar Tales* Book to Support Grammar and
Language Development in Children

Jessica Habib

Illustrated by Carina Ward

Routledge
Taylor & Francis Group

LONDON AND NEW YORK

Cover image: Carina Ward

First published 2023
by Routledge
4 Park Square, Milton Park, Abingdon, Oxon OX14 4RN

and by Routledge
605 Third Avenue, New York, NY 10158

Routledge is an imprint of the Taylor & Francis Group, an informa business

British Library Cataloguing-in-Publication Data
A catalogue record for this book is available from the British Library

Library of Congress Cataloging-in-Publication Data
A catalog record for this book has been requested

ISBN: 978-1-032-27434-8 (pbk)
ISBN: 978-1-003-29274-6 (ebk)

DOI: 10.4324/9781003292746

Typeset in Calibri
by Apex CoVantage, LLC

A Day at the Beach

Pete

Belle

Jem

It is a hot day. Belle touches yellow sand.

Pete finds a little shell.

Jem builds a big sandcastle.

They hear quiet waves.

Belle sees grey sky.

Jem has a red bucket. She sees long fish.

Pete sees fast crabs. He has a green snorkel.

They feel cold water.

Belle hears loud thunder.

She feels heavy rain.

They watch the big storm. They snuggle in soft towels.

Dad drives the fast car.

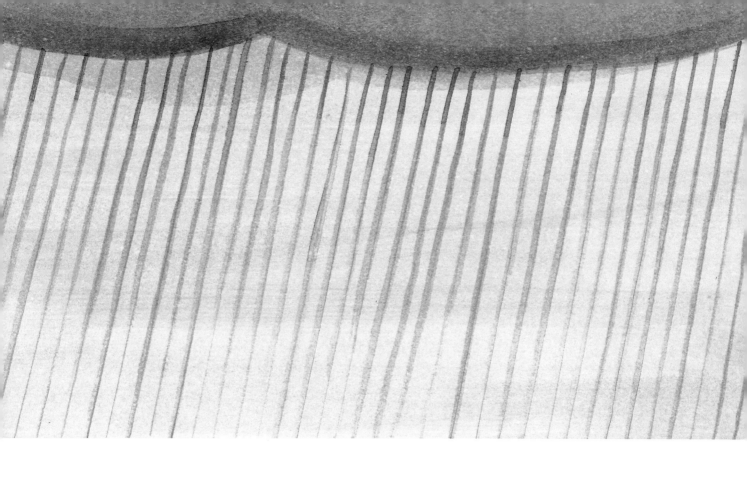

Pete gets his green snorkel.
Jem gets her blue snorkel.
Belle gets her little bucket.

They have a loud bath!